LILLENAS® DRAMA

D1225632

Reality Check

Sketches Focused on Being Real

by Martha Bolton

Lillenas® PUBLISHING COMPANY

KANSAS CITY, MO 64141

Dedication

To my new daughter-in-law, Crystal.
Welcome to our family.

Acknowledgments

A special thank you to:

My husband, Russ, for being my best friend

My family—Russ II, Matt, Nicole, Kiana, Tony, and Crystal—for all the laughter and joy they bring into my life

My "adopted" mother, Diantha Ain, for her encouragement and love

Linda Aleahmad and Mary Scott for always reminding me I've got a deadline, and for being friends by every definition

Kim Messer for the terrific job she's doing in carrying on Paul Miller's vision for church drama

And finally to Paul Miller . . . who started it all

Contents

Preface

The world has heard all the Christian clichés. They've been told the pat answers to their problems. They've watched how some of us have acted when a fellow believer has fallen out of grace.

People need real. Christ was real. He met people where they were. He knew they needed a Savior, not more accusers. When the woman who was caught in adultery was about to be stoned, Jesus didn't join the others and start pitching rocks in her direction. He reminded the crowd of their own sins, then told the woman, "Neither do I condemn thee: go, and sin no more." Instead of making an example out of her, He used her to give the world an example of His unconditional love. Her sin was real, but so was His love and forgiveness.

This collection of sketches reminds us all to take a reality check. It's about taking what we say, what God says, and making it genuine. The sketches are easily staged and require few props. They can be performed singularly or as a full evening's entertainment. I hope you'll have fun with them, learn from them, and above all else, realize that drama is an art—it can even be a ministry—but our best acting belongs on the stage, not in our lives.

Sunday Dinner

A comedy sketch about backbiting

Characters:
> KENT
> KELLY
> MARISA
> MIKE
> WAITER or WAITRESS
> INSPECTOR DILLARD, S.H.D. AGENT

Setting:
> A French restaurant, Critique Bistro

Props:
> Notebook and paper
> Table
> Four chairs
> Four menus
> Order pad
> Pen
> Badge with holder
> Sign, CAFÉ PARIS
> Sign, CLOSED

Costumes:
> Waiter attire for WAITER or WAITRESS
> Modern-day wear for others

NOTE: Waiter should speak with a French accent

(Sketch opens with KENT, KELLY, MARISA, and MIKE seated at the table, looking over their menus. WAITER approaches them, pad and pen in hand.)

WAITER: Good afternoon, mademoiselles and messieurs. May I take your order?

KELLY: Do you have any specials?

WAITER: But of course. Today we are serving ze house specialty, Steak Pastor.

KENT: Steak Pastor? What's that?

MIKE (*looking at menu*): Expensive. $24.95.

WAITER: Oui, but monsieur, you are not at ze Taco Bell. Steak Pastor is our finest entree. We begin with ze premium quality pastor, imported from ze best Bible schools. Then we marinate him in various criticisms and complaints until he iz so tender, he just fall off ze fork.

KELLY: That sounds good to me.

WAITER: It's our most popular dish with ze after-church crowd.

KENT (*to* KELLY): You go ahead. I had Steak Pastor last week. What else do you recommend?

WAITER: If you do not wish ze Steak Pastor, then I recommend our Brisket of Choir Director.

MARISA: How's that prepared?

WAITER: We take one choir director, a cut above what the others are serving, dash on some gossip and innuendo, then skewer him and grill over an open fire to your liking.

MARISA: I think I'll have that.

WAITER: Excellent choice, mademoiselle. (*He writes it down.*) And for you, sir? (*Indicates* MIKE)

MIKE: I'm having a hard time deciding between Church Treasurer Florentine and Leg O'Youth Pastor.

WAITER: Ah, yes . . . both superb dishes. Myself? I would go with the Church Treasurer Florentine.

MIKE: It's good, huh?

WAITER: Oui, it iz new, but already it iz one of my favorites. A little chewy, but still very good, very good.

MIKE: All right. I'll give it a try.

(WAITER *writes it down.*)

WAITER (*indicating* KELLY): And for you?

KELLY: To tell you the truth, I'm trying to limit my church staff intake to two or three times a week. Too much cholesterol. Besides, the pastor's been preaching on it lately. I hate conviction. It ruins your appetite. I'll tell you what, do you have any layperson specials?

WAITER: But of course. We have our popular New Member Roast. Very juicy and tender. And the presentation iz so spectacular. We dress it up entirely to your liking. By the time it meets all your specifications, it'll look nothing like it did when we first added it to the menu. And meeting your specifications is what we're all about here at Critique Bistro.

KELLY: That really sounds tempting, but *(pointing to menu)* this looks even better . . . Evangelist Kabobs.

WAITER *(writing it down on his order pad)*: Another most excellent choice.

KENT: Maybe I'll have that too. Is it very filling?

WAITER: I'm so sorry, monsieur, but that iz a problem with most of our entrees. You eat one fellow Christian and an hour later you're wanting to feed on another.

KENT: In that case, I'm going with the Steak Pastor. It says here it's all-you-can-eat.

WAITER: Oui. Chew up all you want, we'll send you more. *(He writes it down.)* Now, would any of you care to begin your meal with a cup of our Deacon DeJour? It iz one of our specialties.

KELLY: Deacon DeJour?

WAITER: A hearty broth featuring a different deacon every day, depending on which one is in ze hot water. Today it iz Deacon Miles.

KENT: Deacon Miles . . . someone was telling me something about him just this morning.

WAITER: See, ze word is spreading so quickly, we can't keep up with the orders.

MIKE: OK, soup all around.

WAITER: Very well.

(As WAITER writes it down, INSPECTOR DILLARD enters.)

INSPECTOR *(to WAITER)*: Inspector Dillard from the S.H.D. *(Flashes badge)* Spiritual Health Department. We've received some complaints about the . . . er . . . food being served here at your bistro.

WAITER: I don't know what it iz you're talking about, officer. Not one of my customers has ever complained . . . at least, not while partaking of it.

INSPECTOR: I'll still need to inspect your kitchen.

WAITER: Inspect away, but I assure you everything is in order. But, please, excuse me for just one moment . . . *(Moves over to the kitchen door. Opens it or mimes the action, then yells inside.)* Code Green! Code Green! Eighty-six the after-church menu! Return to regular!

INSPECTOR: I heard that.

WAITER: Heard what, monsieur?

INSPECTOR: Just what kind of menu items have you been serving here anyway?

WAITER: All right, we have a few specials you won't find at Denny's, but does that make us criminals?

13

INSPECTOR (*picks up menu and reads from it):* Steak Pastor . . . Evangelist Kabobs . . . Leg O'Youth Pastor . . . What kind of restaurant is this?

WAITER: We cater to the church crowd.

INSPECTOR: They eat this stuff?

WAITER: Not all of them. But as you can see, we're doing a healthy business.

INSPECTOR: Not from our standpoint. The S.H.D. rules explicitly state that Christians aren't supposed to feed on each other.

WAITER: They taste just like chicken.

INSPECTOR: Sorry, but we're going to have to shut you down.

WAITER: You can't do that!

INSPECTOR: Watch me.

WAITER: I'll go over your head!

INSPECTOR: Go ahead. (*Pointing heavenward*) He agrees with me. Didn't you read your handbook?

WAITER: I was planning to someday . . .

INSPECTOR: Well, in the handbook (*points heavenward*) He gave us, there are all sorts of scriptures that warn us against backbiting, bearing false witness, and chewing each other up with gossip.

WAITER: OK, so maybe it iz a little fattening . . .

INSPECTOR: It's not fattening, it's wrong.

KELLY: Look, it's not all his fault. We're the ones who ordered it.

WAITER: That's right. Supply and demand.

INSPECTOR: That's true. People who feed on it are just as guilty as the one who serves it. But I'm still gonna have to shut this place down.

KENT: You can't wait until after we eat?

WAITER: The rest of the after-church crowd will be here any minute. Couldn't you come back this evening or, say, tomorrow?

INSPECTOR: Sorry, enough damage has been done already.

MARISA: So this means no Brisket of Choir Director?

MIKE: And no Church Treasurer Florentine?

INSPECTOR: It means you'll have to start changing your dining habits. Eat the things God gave us to eat—like meat and vegetables and fruit. He never intended our diets to be each other.

KELLY: Sounds boring, but I guess we don't really have a choice.

WAITER (to customers): I'm so sorry about all of this.

INSPECTOR (posts the large CLOSED sign): Break God's laws and we have to shut you down.

(KENT, KELLY, MARISA, and MIKE rise to leave.)

KELLY: So what do we do now?

MIKE: Maybe there's a Burger King or something open.

KENT: Yeah. But I was really looking forward to that Steak Pastor.

MARISA: Do you think we could actually make it through one meal without chewing on somebody?

KELLY: It'll be tough, but I'm up for it.

KENT: Me, too, I guess.

(They exit.)

WAITER (to INSPECTOR): Well, I hope you're happy.

INSPECTOR (finishing up paperwork): Just doing my job.

WAITER: I know. To tell you the truth, I was getting a little tired of that menu anyway. I know I was getting tired of that French accent.

INSPECTOR: You're not from France?

WAITER (losing accent): Boise. Hey, I've got it! I'll reopen with Italian cuisine. (In Italian accent) Mama mia, you've simply got to try our Church Secretary Calzoni. (In regular voice) That oughta bring 'em in, yes?

INSPECTOR: You haven't learned anything, have you?

WAITER: OK, then we'll go south of the border. (With a Spanish accent) Good evening, senors and senoritas, welcome to Paco's Place.

INSPECTOR: Do what you want, but you've still got to change your menu.

WAITER (in Spanish accent): Si, senor, how's these? Children's Church Worker Chalupas, Church Janitor Taquitos, Arroz con Drama Director . . .

INSPECTOR: You're still not getting it!

WAITER: Can I help it if I know what people like to eat?

INSPECTOR: It doesn't change the law. You're still closed.

WAITER: OK, we'll go barbeque. (In southern accent) Bubba's Place . . . full slab of Sunday School Director . . . Grilled Pianist Patties, Rotisserie Usher. Ya'll come?!

INSPECTOR: No barbecue, no Italian, and no south of the border. You're out of business!

WAITER: Asian? East Indian? Swedish? *(In Swedish accent)* You haven't lived until you've tasted a Nursery Worker Meatball. *(In regular voice)* C'mon, give me a direction here. I'll try anything. Just don't shut me down.

INSPECTOR: Sorry. It's out of my hands. If I were you, I'd get into another line of work.

(INSPECTOR leaves.)

WAITER: Another line of work? Umph! I've been serving up church gossip for as long as I can remember. I don't know anything else . . . Wait a minute. I could start serving politicians. Yeah! That's it! Deep Fried President, Sautéed Senator, Boiled Congressman and Beans . . . that's perfect! *(He starts to follow* INSPECTOR *offstage.)* Inspector! Inspector! I've got my new menu . . . Politics! There isn't anything in God's Word about chewing up political leaders. *(He pauses for a beat.)* . . . Wait a minute . . . maybe there is . . . but it's just one or two verses. Maybe he hasn't read it. *(He continues to walk offstage.)* Inspector! Oh, Inspector!

Blackout

If There's Anything We Can Do . . .

A comedy sketch about "being there"

Characters:
>FRANK
>CHRISTINE
>BETTY
>MARY ANN CARTER

Setting:
>The front porch of MARY ANN's home

Props:
>Purses for BETTY and CHRISTINE

Costumes:
>Modern-day wear

(Sketch opens with FRANK, CHRISTINE, *and* BETTY *approaching the "front door" of* MARY ANN CARTER. *They knock.* MARY ANN *comes to the door.)*

BETTY *(reading from card):* Mary Ann Carter?

MARY ANN: Yes?

FRANK: We're from the church bereavement committee.

CHRISTINE: We came to offer our condolences in the passing of your husband.

BETTY: We're so sorry.

CHRISTINE: If there's anything we can do . . .

FRANK: Anything at all . . .

BETTY: Please don't hesitate . . .

CHRISTINE: We're here for you.

FRANK: But we can't help you if you don't tell us . . .

BETTY: . . . how we can help.

MARY ANN: Well, there is one thing . . .

FRANK: Yes, of course . . .

BETTY: What is it, dear?

CHRISTINE: We want to help out in any . . .

BETTY: . . . way we can.

FRANK: Think of us as family.

CHRISTINE: More than family.

BETTY *(takes MARY ANN's hand):* We're your brothers and sisters in the Lord.

MARY ANN: Well, you know how much I depended on my Ben . . .

FRANK: Of course.

BETTY: This must be a difficult time for you.

MARY ANN: Since Ben's passing, I've had a little trouble getting around, seeing's how I don't drive and all.

CHRISTINE: Yes . . .

FRANK: Of course . . .

MARY ANN: Well, I was wondering if someone could drive me to the store tomorrow. . . . If that's not too much trouble.

BETTY: Drive you to the store? That's no trouble.

CHRISTINE: No trouble at all.

FRANK: We're just happy we can help.

BETTY: Like we said . . . we're your brothers and sisters in the Lord. . . . wait, did you say tomorrow?

FRANK: Tomorrow's no good for me.

CHRISTINE: Me either.

FRANK: The kids have a soccer game.

CHRISTINE: And I can't change my hair appointment at this late date.

BETTY: I wouldn't want to drive all the way out here alone.

FRANK: Sorry. Tomorrow doesn't seem to be working out.

CHRISTINE: Actually, driving you around is something your husband should be . . . *(Catches herself)* Oh, sorry. But if there's anything else . . .

BETTY: Anything at all . . .

FRANK: We're here for you . . .

CHRISTINE: You just let us know.

BETTY *(to others):* Maybe we can make a dinner for her one night.

MARY ANN: That would be nice.

FRANK *(to* BETTY*):* Do you cook?

BETTY: I don't cook.

CHRISTINE: Well, don't look at me. I haven't cooked in years.

FRANK: How do you feel about going out?

MARY ANN: That's fine.

BETTY: I hate crowds.

CHRISTINE: She's right. And you never know if the service is going to be any good or not.

FRANK: OK, so maybe going out isn't such a good idea.

CHRISTINE: So then, what are we going to do for her?

BETTY: Who? *(A beat)* Oh, yes . . . *(Looks at card)* Mary Ann . . . our dear sister.

FRANK: We're here to help her, remember?

CHRISTINE: That's right.

FRANK *(to* MARY ANN*):* So, if there's anything else . . . anything at all . . .

CHRISTINE: Don't hesitate . . .

BETTY: You need to open up to us.

FRANK: Tell us how we can help you.

MARY ANN: Well, there were quite a few funeral expenses, and you know I'm on a limited . . .

FRANK: Expenses? *(To others)* Did she say expenses?

(Both CHRISTINE *and* BETTY *clutch their purses protectively.)*

CHRISTINE: Sounded like *expenses* to me.

BETTY: Me too.

FRANK *(to* MARY ANN*):* You're meaning expenses as in *expenses?*

MARY ANN: Don't worry about it. I just thought I'd mention it . . .

FRANK: Please, don't get us wrong. We'd love to help.

CHRISTINE: . . . in any way we can.

BETTY: But . . . well, you know . . .

MARY ANN: Actually, I don't think I need anything right now.

FRANK: You're sure?

CHRISTINE: Because we can't help if you don't tell us.

MARY ANN: No, really, I'm fine.

BETTY: Well, you know, if you need anything . . .

CHRISTINE: Anything at all.

FRANK: We're here for you.

MARY ANN *(halfheartedly):* Thanks.

CHRISTINE: We want you to think of us as family.

BETTY: Better than family.

MARY ANN: I'm fine, really.

FRANK: All right, if you're sure.

MARY ANN: Thanks for stopping by. *(She closes the door.)*

FRANK *(marks off her name in his notebook):* Well, one down, six more to go.

BETTY: I sure love this ministry.

FRANK: I really think it's our calling.

CHRISTINE: So, who's next?

FRANK *(reading from list):* Duane Nicholson. Lost his wife three days ago.

BETTY: What a shame.

CHRISTINE: Let's hurry over there.

FRANK: I'm sure there's something we can do for him.

CHRISTINE: I just hope he's more open than Mary Ann and lets us help.

BETTY: Yes, because we want to help . . .

CHRISTINE: . . . in any way we can.

FRANK: Because we're family.

BETTY: Better than family.

CHRISTINE: We're his brothers and sisters . . . in the Lord.

Blackout

In-Flight Entertainment

A sketch about honesty in marriage

Characters:
> BERNADETTE
> HARVEY
> MALCOLM

Setting:
> The inside of an airplane

Props:
> Three chairs
> Airline ticket
> Magazine

Costumes:
> Modern-day wear

(*Sketch opens with* MALCOLM *seated in the middle chair, reading a magazine.* BERNADETTE *and* HARVEY *approach as if walking down the aisle of an airplane.*)

BERNADETTE (*reading "seat numbers"*): Row 10, 11 . . . ah, here we go, row 12. Seats A and C.

HARVEY: Uh-oh.

BERNADETTE: What?

HARVEY: Seats A and C.

BERNADETTE: Yeah, so?

HARVEY: There's someone sitting in B.

BERNADETTE: I see that. Well, maybe he'll move.

HARVEY: Yeah.

(*A beat*)

BERNADETTE: . . . Well?

HARVEY: Well, what?

BERNADETTE: Ask him.

HARVEY: You ask him. Why do I always have to ask?

BERNADETTE: Just ask.

HARVEY: Excuse me, sir . . .

MALCOLM: No.

HARVEY: Excuse me?

MALCOLM: If you're wanting me to move, the answer's no. I purposely request-
ed a middle seat, and since the plane is full, I'm staying right here.

BERNADETTE: Between us?

MALCOLM: Right here.

HARVEY (*to* BERNADETTE): Don't worry about it. Let's just sit down. You want
the window or the aisle?

BERNADETTE: The window, I guess. (*She gives the man an irritated look, then scoots
over him to the window. She sits for a beat before popping back up.*) I'd rather
have the aisle. (*She scoots back over the man again, much to his chagrin. Finally, everyone is seated and* BERNADETTE *and* HARVEY *talk "around"* MALCOLM
throughout the remainder of the sketch.)

HARVEY: I can't believe you messed up the reservations again.

BERNADETTE: Me? Now this is my fault too?

HARVEY: You booked them, didn't you?

BERNADETTE: The ticket agent knew we were Mr. and Mrs. She should have
known we'd want to sit together.

HARVEY (*aside*): Actually, I might enjoy the peace and quiet.

BERNADETTE: What was that?

HARVEY: Nothing.

BERNADETTE: Well, how are we supposed to talk now when you're all the way
over there and I'm over here?

MALCOLM (*looking up from magazine, irritated*): You're doing a good job of it so
far. (*He goes back to reading.*)

HARVEY (*to* BERNADETTE): How long did you say this flight was again?

BERNADETTE: Too long.

HARVEY: So what do you think they're serving for dinner?

BERNADETTE: Probably a box lunch.

HARVEY: I want your cookie.

BERNADETTE: What if I want my cookie?

HARVEY: You never want your cookie.

BERNADETTE: I do today.

HARVEY: You're just saying that because I said I want it.

BERNADETTE: I want my cookie.

HARVEY: You're doing this to irritate me.

BERNADETTE: No, I'm not. It's my cookie and I feel like a cookie today.

(A beat)

HARVEY: You're just saying that.

MALCOLM: Oh, for heaven's sake, you can have *my* cookie! Now, do you mind . . . ?

BERNADETTE: He doesn't want your cookie.

HARVEY: Yes I do.

BERNADETTE: No, you don't. This man's being rude.

MALCOLM: I'm being rude?

(MALCOLM *returns to reading his magazine as he eats his cookie to the dismay of* HARVEY, *then . . .*)

BERNADETTE: Harvey, I'm cold.

HARVEY: Ask the flight attendant for a blanket.

BERNADETTE: People cough on those blankets. Who knows how many germs are living on them.

HARVEY: So what do you want me to do? Go tell the pilot to turn up the heat?

BERNADETTE: Would you really do that for me?

HARVEY: No! I can't go into the cockpit. That's against federal regulations.

BERNADETTE: If you loved me, that wouldn't matter.

HARVEY: You want me to walk into the cockpit and tell the pilot to adjust the thermostat just for you?

BERNADETTE: You did it at Sears.

HARVEY: That was different. You were making a scene refusing to get out of the blanket display and the manager was there anyway.

BERNADETTE (*starts to cry*): You don't love me anymore.

HARVEY: Of course I do, honey.

MALCOLM (*takes off his jacket*): Here, lady, put this on.

BERNADETTE: You really mean it?

MALCOLM: If it'll shut you up . . .

BERNADETTE (*to* HARVEY): See, why can't you be more giving like this man. I bet his wife . . .

MALCOLM: I'm not married.

HARVEY (*to* BERNADETTE): You're not exactly the perfect wife yourself, you know. When's the last time you cooked a meal?

BERNADETTE: I don't know.

HARVEY: I do. I'm still paying on the emergency room bill. It's not cheap getting four stomachs pumped!

BERNADETTE: You're the one who wanted a large family! And do you think for one minute I enjoy your awful snoring?

HARVEY: I don't snore.

BERNADETTE: It vibrates the walls so bad, every morning I've got to rehang all the pictures.

HARVEY: OK, if we're listing aggravations, that thing you do with your teeth is pretty irritating.

BERNADETTE: What thing?

HARVEY: That grinding noise.

BERNADETTE: I don't grind.

MALCOLM: I'm afraid you do, ma'am. It's been getting on my nerves too.

HARVEY AND BERNADETTE (*in unison*): We gave you a chance to move!

MALCOLM: I didn't say I was ready to toss you off the plane. I just said it was irritating. So where're you two headed anyway?

BERNADETTE: A marriage retreat.

MALCOLM: Well, all I can say is you both could sure use it.

HARVEY: Use it? We're teaching it!

(*As* MALCOLM *shakes his head and returns to reading his magazine . . .*)

BERNADETTE: Come on, Harvey, I'm still freezing. Go talk to the pilot.

HARVEY: I told you that's out of the question! And I don't snore.

BERNADETTE: Yes you do.

HARVEY: No I don't!

BERNADETTE: Yes . . . you . . . do . . .

HARVEY: No, I don't . . .

Blackout

High-Fashion Christian

Characters:
    PAULINE CHAVINSKY: *fashion show moderator*
    CYNTHIA: *model Christian (may also be played by a male), nonspeaking role*

Setting:
    A fashion show

Props:
    Podium
    Fashion show script for PAULINE to refer to from time to time

Costumes:
    Fashionable modern wear for PAULINE
    Body armor as described in sketch (for CYNTHIA)

(Sketch opens with PAULINE at the podium. The fashion show is in progress. CYNTHIA appears and proceeds to model her attire as PAULINE gives the description.)

PAULINE: And now for our next ensemble. Cynthia is wearing what all model Christians will be wearing this season—the full armor of God. We'll begin with the breastplate of righteousness. Yes, believe it or not, righteousness is back in style again. For the truly fashion savvy, though, it never went out of vogue. Notice how the breastplate fully covers the heart. That's because righteousness serves as a protection against those things that would harden or turn a heart against God. The metal is an easy-to-care-for polish n'wear metal that can also give you a great tan when the sun hits it just right. It's a one-size-fits-all and offers no protection in the back because, quite frankly, that's not the direction a model Christian is supposed to be headed in. Maybe that's why it comes in all colors except yellow. *(Pause)* Now, for those of you who've been wondering how to gird your loins this year, wonder no more. Truth Loin Wear exploded onto the fashion scene in shows both in New York and Paris and is now sweeping the rest of the world. Unlike tight-fitting designer jeans, Truth Loin Wear gives your body a chance to breathe.

    And knowing the truth is what breathing easy is all about. *(Pause)* For those of you sick and tired of combating those bad hair days, your battle is over. Our helmet of salvation will give you victory over the most unruly follicles of life. *(Pause)* Now, everyone knows that accessories make the outfit, and for this ensemble we recommend the sword of the Spirit. Unlike a real sword, which would require a license to carry and would never make it past the metal detector at most airports, the sword of the Spirit is simply the Word of God. But don't be fooled. The Word of God, though, is as sharp as a two-edged sword and can penetrate even the most stone-cold heart. *(Pause)* Another popular accessory for our ensemble is the shield of faith. Not only does this help to tie the outfit together, but it will also quench the fiery darts of the enemy. And anyone who's seen what a fiery dart can do to polyester won't want to leave home without this shield. *(Pause)* Last, but not least, comes the footwear. How is the well-dressed Christian shodding their feet this season? With the preparation of the gospel of peace, of course. Nothing shods like the gospel of peace shods. Not leather, not canvas, not even rattlesnake skin. The gospel of peace also comes in all those hard-to-fit sizes and is so comfortable, you'll wonder why you didn't shod your feet in it years ago. *(Pause)* If you'd like more information or would like to order the full armor of God, you can do so by going to www.Galatians6:13-17.com, or just look it up in your Bible. *(Pause)* So put on the whole armor of God and wear what all well-dressed Christians will be wearing this season because God is one designer who never goes out of style.

Blackout

The Prayer Request

Characters:
> BETH
> LARAMIE

Setting:
> Church foyer following the service

Props:
> Large notebook overflowing with loose papers
> Pen (in BETH's pocket)

Costumes:
> Modern-day wear

(Sketch opens with BETH *and* LARAMIE *walking onstage as though church has just let out and they've run into each other in the foyer.)*

LARAMIE: Beth . . . how're ya doing?

BETH: Great, Laramie. And yourself?

LARAMIE: Good. Good. *(Pause)* Wasn't that a wonderful sermon?

BETH: Always is. He's the best.

LARAMIE *(indicating notebook):* Watcha got there?

BETH: You mean this?

LARAMIE: Yeah.

BETH: Oh, it's nothing.

LARAMIE: I see you with it every Sunday. Why would you carry nothing to church every single Sunday?

BETH: If you must know, it's my . . . well, you know how someone catches you off guard, tells you about a problem they're having and you don't know what to say, so you say "I'll be praying for you"?

LARAMIE: Of course. The standard answer.

BETH: Well, when that happens to me, I write down the person's name and the problem in this notebook. *(Some papers fall out. She doesn't bother to pick them up, but when* LARAMIE *tries to help . . .)* Don't worry about 'em. I've got plenty. Anyway, as I was saying, I write them down so I'll be able to . . .

LARAMIE: Pray for them?

BETH: No . . . keep track of them.

LARAMIE: You don't pray for them?

BETH: I honestly plan to. But I get so busy. You know how that is.

LARAMIE: But don't you realize when you say you're going to pray, someone's counting on you to do it?

BETH: Of course I do. That's why I keep all . . . *(looks at file on the ground)* OK, most of them in this notebook. *(She drops a few more.)*

LARAMIE: You're not going to pick up those either?

BETH: God knows what they are.

LARAMIE: And you should too. *(Bends over and picks up one of the papers and reads from it)* Mrs. Mildred Smith . . .

BETH: Mildred Smith . . . Mildred Smith . . . Oh yes, I remember her. She wants me to pray for some health thing . . . and I'm planning on doing it. Soon. Very soon.

LARAMIE: I take it you didn't hear she died last week.

BETH: She did?

LARAMIE *(nods)*: Her funeral was Thursday.

BETH *(takes the paper and throws it down again)*: See, I don't need that one after all.

LARAMIE: I don't think you understand this prayer request thing. *(Picks up another one and reads name from it)* What about Mrs. Nancy Foley . . . ?

BETH: Foley? Oh, I definitely remember her. She wanted me to pray for her marriage.

LARAMIE: And did you?

BETH: No, but I'm going to just . . .

LARAMIE: They're divorced.

BETH: How was I to know the marriage would disintegrate that quickly?

LARAMIE *(looking over request)*: This prayer request was dated three years ago.

BETH: I told you I've been busy.

LARAMIE: You know, God does answer prayer, but somebody has to pray it first.

BETH *(takes one of the papers out of her notebook, defensively)*: OK, here's one who wasn't hurt by my not praying. Keven Hendricks . . . he asked me to pray for God to give him a better paying job so he could make his mortgage payments.

LARAMIE: And of course you didn't pray.

BETH: Right, but now that they've foreclosed on his house, he doesn't have to worry about that prayer request anymore. *(She wads up the paper and tosses it aside.)*

LARAMIE: Beth, I don't think that's the answer he wanted.

BETH *(takes out another paper):* And remember the Hendricksons?

LARAMIE: Of course. *(Takes paper from BETH and reads it)* They wanted traveling mercies for their summer vacation. But you didn't get around to praying for them either, did you?

BETH: They made it back, didn't they?

LARAMIE: Not with their car. It got hijacked!

BETH: They only wanted me to pray for them to make it back safely. *(Indicating prayer request form)* There's nothing on here about a car.

LARAMIE: Don't you know when someone's asked you to pray for them, you might be the only one they've asked?

BETH: Hey, don't blame it all on me. People can pray for themselves, too, you know. It's not all my responsibility.

LARAMIE: True, but Jesus said, "When two or three agree, asking anything in my name . . ."

BETH: Oh, all right. I see your point.

LARAMIE: God hears every prayer, but when we help someone else pray for their need, it's even more powerful.

BETH: Guess I've been letting a lot of people down.

LARAMIE: Well, it's never too late to start praying now.

BETH: Right. *(Starts picking up the papers on the floor)* These people are depending on me. And I'm going to go home tonight and pray for each and every one of them. *(One of the requests catches her eye.)* Umm . . . I wonder whatever happened to Mitzi Pryor. Did she ever have that baby she always wanted?

LARAMIE: Sure did.

BETH: Maybe I should drop off a diaper bag or something.

LARAMIE: The baby just graduated from med school. In fact, that "baby" is the mother of six now.

BETH: Boy, when God answers prayer, He really answers it, doesn't He?

LARAMIE: If we pray it, He hears it.

BETH: You know, maybe someone should invent a self-expiring prayer request form. As soon as God answers it, it disintegrates in your hands. Then you'll know you won't have to keep carrying it around.

LARAMIE: That's not a bad idea, but in the meantime . . .

BETH: I know. I know. Pray for the ones I've got.

LARAMIE: Those people are counting on you.

BETH: And this time, I'm not going to let them down. *(Reads off a few more forms as she exits)* Cliff McKinley . . . um, I wonder how his court case ever turned out. And Jean Rutherford . . . this is a two-year-old request. She's got to be out of surgery by now. And . . .

Blackout

Only Skin Deep

A sketch about hiding God's Word in your heart

Characters:
> CURT
> AMY

Setting:
> Just outside a seedy tattoo parlor

Props:
> None needed

Costumes:
> Modern-day wear for AMY
> A loose T-shirt, knee-length shorts, shoes, and socks for CURT. He also should have tattoos of scripture written on various parts of his body (as indicated throughout the script). Whatever is used to accomplish this look should be safe and easily removable. Real tattooing is not recommended.

(Sketch opens with CURT just stepping out of the tattoo parlor as AMY walks by.)

AMY: Curt. Hi. What're you doing downtown?

CURT: Well, I did it.

AMY: Did what?

CURT: What our youth pastor said to do. I engraved God's Word on my heart . . . Well, not exactly on my heart . . .

AMY *(slowly):* Curt . . . what have you done?

CURT *(proudly):* Got a tattoo of the Bible.

AMY: The Bible?

CURT: From Genesis all the way to the maps!

AMY: You tattooed the whole Bible on your body?

CURT: Of course not. You think I'm a fanatic or something? I left off the genealogies.

AMY: Tell me you're joking.

CURT: This one begat that one who begat this one. I'd have to put on a few more pounds to fit all that in.

AMY: I mean, tell me you're joking about the whole thing. You didn't really tattoo the whole Bible on you, did you?

CURT: Don't worry. It's the King James Version. You know, I don't know why I didn't think about this sooner. I wouldn't have had to memorize all those scriptures for youth group, Vacation Bible School, Awanas, Sunday School class . . .

AMY: But that's what you're supposed to do—memorize God's Word. Get it in your heart, not in your epidermis.

CURT: There's no reason to swear.

AMY: I wasn't swearing. Epidermis means your skin. God's Word belongs in your heart, not in your skin.

CURT: You're just saying that because you know I'm going to win all the Bible quizzes from now on.

AMY: I'm saying that because you look ridiculous.

CURT: I've got a scripture for you . . . *(Starts searching his arms and legs)* I know it's here somewhere. Now, where did I put the Psalms?

AMY: You haven't been getting enough sleep lately, have you, Curt?

CURT: I've been sleeping like a baby. You know what they say—when you stand on God's Word, you're anxious for nothing. And that's exactly what I'm doing. *(Shows her the bottom of his feet)* . . . Jude.

AMY: You need help, Curt.

CURT: You're not seeing the big picture, Amy. This is all about spiritual growth. I can now have devotions wherever I'm at—even in the shower!

AMY: Most people don't have their devotions underwater.

CURT: Well, I can! And see here . . . *(Shows left shoulder)* Fluorescent. I don't even have to turn the light on to read my Bible. That's the Book of Judges. Pretty cool, huh?

AMY: How much did all this cost?

CURT: It wasn't cheap, but it's worth every penny. He was going to throw in a concordance, but I was starting to get a little dizzy. But here, check this out . . . *(He lowers the back of his shirt collar, revealing his right shoulder.)* Read it.

AMY *(reading):* "Get thee behind me, Satan."

CURT *(laughs):* Isn't that great?! I put it back there so he could read it. Clever, huh?

AMY: Uh . . . yeah, I . . . guess so. *(Indicating the side of his neck)* So, which scripture is this?

CURT: Oh, that's nothing. Just freckles.

AMY: Well, I've got to hand it to you, Curt, this brings a whole new meaning to "witness wear." But it had to be painful.

CURT (*proudly*): I'm just suffering for the Lord.

AMY: But, Curt, didn't you hear me? God didn't tell us to tattoo His Word on our bodies. He wants us to engrave it on our hearts.

CURT: Whoa, wait a minute. No one's tattooing my heart! At least not while I'm still using it. Do you have any idea how much that'd hurt? Besides, how would I ever read it?

AMY: Not our physical hearts. Our emotional ones. Tattooing God's Word on our bodies isn't the same as getting it inside of here (*indicates heart*) and making it a part of our life.

CURT: So you're saying I didn't have to go through all this?

AMY: You do tend to go to extremes, Curt.

CURT (*looking over tattoos*): You wouldn't happen to have an eraser on you, would you?

AMY: I think it's going to take more than an eraser to remove all that.

CURT: Well, to tell you the truth, it'll just take a little soap and water. It's temporary. I wanted to see if I liked it before I did the real thing.

AMY: Whew! That's a relief!

CURT: I'll just wash all this off and go back to memorizing the scriptures like I should have been doing all along. (*Pause*) I sure am glad I ran in to you today.

AMY: Me too . . .

CURT: Yeah, next week they were scheduled to start the real thing, beginning with Psalm 119.

AMY: The longest chapter in the Bible? Now that would've hurt! (*Leading* CURT *offstage*) C'mon, let's go look for some soap.

Blackout

Originally written for Ron Luce Ministries.

The Mission

Characters:

    LOLA: *movie star*
    BERNIE: *Hollywood agent*
    REV. CARMELIA: *mission director*

Setting:

    Downtown mission

Props:

    Ladle
    Cell phone
    Serving table
    Serving dish
    Camera, with flash

Costumes:

    LOLA, an actress and legend in her own eyes, should be way overdressed for mission work.
    REV. CARMELIA should be dressed as a minister.
    BERNIE is dressed like a Hollywood agent.

(Sketch opens with LOLA talking into the cell phone as she "serves" the homeless. She dishes out a scoop per person. The food and the line are left to the audience's imagination. LOLA tries to be discreet and not let the homeless hear her phone conversation, but sometimes she can't help herself.)

LOLA *(into cell phone):* . . . Well? You'd better have a good explanation. *(Pause)* So, take a side street! *(Pause)* This is not what I agreed to! *(Pause)* All you said was this would be a great photo op. That's all. You never said anything about my having to stay here and serve! *(She dishes out another scoop, as if serving the next in line.)* There you go, honey. *(Pause)* God bless you too. *(Into cell phone)* Do you realize some of these people haven't bathed in weeks! *(Pause)* Yes, I know they're homeless, but they could have the decency to walk through some sprinklers or something! *(Serves another "scoop." Pause.)* Here. I hope you like beef . . . or is that chicken? *(Pause)* Well, whatever it is, I hope you like it. *(Pause)* Oh, rats! *(As if to person in line)* Uh, sorry, it's not rats. Beef or chicken—that's all we serve. *(Into cell phone)* One of my acrylics broke off! Must've fallen into that last scoop. *(Pause)* See, I told you I'm not cut out for this kind of work. It's too hands-on. Now, get down here before that lady figures out the fingernails she's chewing on aren't her own! How I ever let you talk me into this in the first place is beyond me. *(Pause)* Good for my career? How can you say that? There aren't any producers down here or network executives. *(Pause)* OK, there's that one, but he's outside talking to a streetlight. What can he do for me?

(Rev. Carmelia *enters.*)

Rev. Carmelia: So, how's it going, Lola?

Lola: Fine, Reverend, fine.

Rev. Carmelia: Well, we sure appreciate you giving your time to the mission like this.

Lola: Oh, Reverend, I couldn't think of eating Thanksgiving dinner knowing there are those among us going to bed hungry. *(Whispering into phone)* Bernie, why aren't you here with the video? I'll never be able to fake that kind of sincerity again! *(Pause)* Yeah, I guess you're right. I'm an actress. I can fake anything.

Rev. Carmelia: What's that?

Lola: Uh . . . I said, if there's anything else I can do, please don't hesitate to ask.

Rev. Carmelia: No, no. You've already given so much.

Lola: Reverend, these people are giving me so much more than I'm giving them. *(Smiles oh so sincerely.)*

(Rev. Carmelia *gives her a nod and a slight smile back, then exits.*)

Lola *(into cell phone):* We're talking germs, Bernie! Only God knows what they're giving me! I'm telling you, Bernie, if I come down with a fatal disease and die, you're fired! And you're off my Christmas list too! *(Pause)* What's that? You're pulling into the driveway now? Well, it's about time! *(Drops another scoop of food onto another imaginary plate, then smiles at them)* Enjoy! There's plenty more where that came from. *(She looks down at the serving tray and grimaces.)* . . . Unfortunately.

(Bernie *rushes in, camera in hand.*)

Bernie: Lola, sweetheart . . . *(He approaches her, arms outstretched.)*

Lola: Finally! Take your picture and let's get outta here!

Bernie: It's gotta look real, Lola. It can't look staged, you know.

Lola: But it is staged.

Bernie: I know, but it can't look it. You'll need to be serving them or something.

Lola *(she poses, ladle raised):* Come on, snap it!

Bernie: Perfect! That's perfect!

(Lola *goes through a series of poses as* Bernie's *camera is flashing away.*)

Lola: You're getting my best side, aren't you, Bernie?

BERNIE: Always do, Lola. Always do.

(He takes a few more pictures, then . . .)

LOLA: OK, that's enough. Let's get out of here.

BERNIE: You're forgetting, we signed you up for two hours.

LOLA: Well, it's been that.

BERNIE *(looks at watch):* Eighteen minutes.

LOLA: I have 18 minutes left?

BERNIE: You've only been here 18 minutes.

LOLA: So, let 'em take it out of my paycheck.

(They start to leave just as REV. CARMELIA enters.)

REV. CARMELIA: Leaving so soon?

LOLA: I'm so sorry, Reverend, but I completely forgot I have another engagement.

REV. CARMELIA: Oh, that's a shame. We're so shorthanded, we were really counting on you.

LOLA: Believe me, if there was anything I could do to rearrange my . . .

BERNIE: Well, maybe there is . . .

LOLA *(glaring at BERNIE):* No, no . . . there's just no way at this late date.

BERNIE: I suppose you're right. They are counting on you . . .

LOLA: Yes, they're counting on me. The, uh . . . *(obviously making it up)* Helping Hands Mission. Wonderful people, wonderful people.

REV. CARMELIA: You're helping over there this afternoon?

LOLA: I guess I have a problem with saying no.

REV. CARMELIA: The Helping Hands Mission, that's on . . .

(Simultaneously)

LOLA: Fifth Street.   BERNIE: Bradley Avenue.

REV. CARMELIA: Actually, I believe it's Third and Main.

BERNIE: Third and Main. Of course.

LOLA: We always get lost going over there.

REV. CARMELIA: Well, you won't today! I'm headed over there myself. Just follow me.

LOLA: Uh . . . follow . . .

BERNIE: . . . you?

LOLA: You want us to follow you?

REV. CARMELIA: Sure. *(He puts his arms around both of them as he leads them off-stage.)* Wow . . . two missions in one day. Why can't there be more people in the world like Lola Duvan—so warm, so giving, so real . . .

BERNIE: She's something, all right.

LOLA: I'm just doing what I can to make this world a better place. *(She leans behind* REV. CARMELIA's *back and catches* BERNIE's *eye.)* You'd better have film in that camera!

Blackout

The Contract

A sketch about commitment

Characters:
> CHRISTINE
> TONY
> ATTORNEY
> PREACHER

Setting:
> Wedding chapel

Props:
> Contract and several other pieces of paper (in ATTORNEY's pocket)
> Wedding ceremony book

Costumes:
> Appropriate wedding attire

SFX:
> Music—suggested "Wedding March" and "Recessional"

(Sketch opens with TONY *and* ATTORNEY *standing at the front of the chapel,* PREACHER *is across from them, open book in hand. "Wedding March" begins.* CHRISTINE *enters and walks down the aisle. She joins her groom and the ceremony is underway.)*

PREACHER: Dearly beloved, we are gathered here today in the presence of these witnesses to join together Christine and Tony in holy matrimony.

CHRISTINE *(aside to* TONY*)*: I love you, honey . . .

TONY: I love you too, sweetie . . .

CHRISTINE: . . . with all my heart.

TONY: Yes, I know.

(A beat)

CHRISTINE: Well . . . ?

TONY: Well what?

CHRISTINE: Aren't you going to say you love me with all your heart?

TONY: I said I love you.

CHRISTINE: You didn't say with all your heart. I said I loved you with all my heart, but you didn't say it.

TONY: You're making a scene, dear.

CHRISTINE: It's important to me that you love me with all your heart.

TONY: We can talk about this after we're married.

CHRISTINE: We need to talk about it now.

TONY (to PREACHER): I'm sorry. She gets this way sometimes.

CHRISTINE: I get what way?

TONY: Stub . . . I mean, insistent.

CHRISTINE: I'm not asking for anything I don't deserve.

TONY: I know, but ask later. We'll talk about it . . . sometime before our 10th anniversary. I promise. (To PREACHER) Please, go on.

CHRISTINE (to PREACHER): Don't say another word until this issue is resolved.

TONY (to audience): Sorry, folks. I don't know what's gotten into her. She used to be so understanding.

CHRISTINE: Well, excuse me if I'm not into one-sided relationships.

TONY: Why should you care if I love you with 100 percent of my heart, 80 percent of my heart, or 60 percent of my heart? As long as you've got the majority of it, what difference does it make?

CHRISTINE: What difference does it make?! You've got 100 percent of my heart. It's only fair that you be totally committed to me too.

ATTORNEY: Uh . . . excuse me, but I'm afraid he can't do that.

CHRISTINE: Of course he can. He . . . (Stops for a moment, then realizes she doesn't know the person standing next to TONY. Indicates ATTORNEY.) Who's he?

TONY: Who?

CHRISTINE (indicating ATTORNEY again): Him.

TONY: Him?

CHRISTINE: Yes. If he's the ring bearer, we waited a lot longer than I thought to get married.

TONY: That's just my attorney.

CHRISTINE: Your attorney?

TONY: Don't worry. He's not staying for the reception.

CHRISTINE: And just why do you think you needed an attorney at our wedding?

ATTORNEY: I'm here to make sure the contract is in order.

CHRISTINE: What contract?

TONY: The standard Rights to Your Heart contract.

CHRISTINE: You mean our donor cards?

ATTORNEY: No. *(Pulls contract out of pocket)* This contract. Now, we only have one basic problem and that's with Section 1064 of the Marriage Code, the Commitment Clause. That's where the party of the first part and the party of the second part pledge 100 percent of their hearts to each other. We have some, uh, reservations, that's all.

PREACHER: You folks do know I charge by the hour, don't you?

CHRISTINE *(to ATTORNEY and TONY)*: What kind of reservations?

ATTORNEY: Well, for one thing, the way the contract reads now . . . the party of the first part . . . *(indicating TONY)* that's him . . . is to pledge his entire heart to the party of the second part . . . that's you.

CHRISTINE: Yes. So? I have no problems pledging my whole heart.

ATTORNEY: But he can't pledge his. That's simply out of the question!

CHRISTINE: I thought we already went over this, Tony.

TONY: I know. But I don't commit to anything, not officially anyway, until it's been checked out by my attorney.

CHRISTINE: So exactly what kind of commitment are you planning on making to me, Tony?

ATTORNEY: Funny you should ask. We just happen to have the new vows right here. *(He pulls another paper from his pocket and hands it to PREACHER.)*

PREACHER: Then I can continue now?

ATTORNEY: With those vows, yes, please . . .

PREACHER *(reading from paper)*: Milk, bread, prunes, Preparation . . .

ATTORNEY *(grabs papers)*: My shopping list. Sorry. *(He reaches into his pocket and takes out another paper and hands it to PREACHER.)* Here . . .

PREACHER: You're sure these are the vows you're agreeing to?

ATTORNEY: That's them.

PREACHER *(reading from new paper)*: Very well, please repeat after me . . . I, Tony, pledge my love and most of my heart to thee, Christine . . .

TONY: I, Tony, pledge my love and most of . . .

CHRISTINE: Wait a minute! I'm not getting married this way!

PREACHER: I can't say that I blame her.

CHRISTINE: I want a real commitment from you, Tony.

TONY: But, Christine, sometimes I'll want you around and sometimes I won't. It doesn't mean I don't love you. I just need my freedom.

CHRISTINE: I'm not settling for that, Tony!

ATTORNEY: Look, we've done all the calculations, and the best we figure we can do is 54 percent of his heart.

CHRISTINE: I want 100 percent.

ATTORNEY: Sixty-three percent. Take it or leave it.

CHRISTINE: One hundred percent.

ATTORNEY: Then, there's no contract.

CHRISTINE: Tony . . . you want to speak for yourself here?

TONY: Honey, I love you. You know that. But I have to keep some of my heart for myself, my career, friends, parties. I need you to be OK with that.

CHRISTINE: I deserve more from you, Tony. I'm committing to you everything I own, everything I am.

TONY: That's your nature. You're better at commitments than I am.

ATTORNEY: All right . . . how 'bout 74 percent. That's as high as we can go.

CHRISTINE: If you really love me, you'll make it 100.

(TONY and ATTORNEY confer.)

TONY: Eighty-six percent.

ATTORNEY: No other girl has ever gotten that much from him. I think he's serious.

CHRISTINE: Make a real commitment, Tony.

TONY: It's all or nothing?

ATTORNEY: Tony, as your attorney, I must advise you that . . .

PREACHER (to ATTORNEY): Oh, hush up!

TONY: Carry on with the ceremony, Preacher.

(ATTORNEY in frustration rips up the contract.)

PREACHER: Finally! Do you, Tony, agree to be 100 percent committed to Christine?

TONY: I do.

PREACHER: And do you, Christine, agree to be 100 percent committed to Tony?

CHRISTINE: I do.

PREACHER: Then by the power vested in me, I now pronounce you man and wife. You may kiss the bride. *(They kiss and exit to the recessional music.)*

PREACHER: See, that wasn't so bad.

ATTORNEY: So that's what it means to be totally committed to someone?

PREACHER: It's like the commitment I made to God some 35 years ago. It had to be 100 percent, or it wouldn't have been real.

ATTORNEY *(in the direction of* TONY *and* CHRISTINE): I guess Tony did the right thing. But a commitment like that would sure put us divorce attorneys out of business.

PREACHER: And just imagine what our churches would be like if people made that kind of a commitment to God. *(Beat)* Care for some wedding cake?

ATTORNEY: Don't mind if I do, Preacher. Don't mind if I do.

Blackout

Originally written for Ron Luce Ministries.

Casting Stones

A comedy sketch about judging others

Characters:
>   MOSHEM
>   HAKIAM

Setting:
>   At a well outside the city

Props:
>   A bag of "rocks"
>   Bucket
>   Well with ledge sturdy enough to sit on

Costumes:
>   Bible time clothing

(Sketch opens with HAKIAM *onstage drawing some water from the well.* MOSHEM *rushes onstage with the bag of rocks over his shoulder. The rocks should be visible over the top of the bag.)*

MOSHEM: Where is everybody?

HAKIAM: Who do you search for, my friend?

MOSHEM: Heard there was to be a stoning today.

HAKIAM: No. No stoning.

MOSHEM: But that woman, the one they caught in adultery? The whole town was talking about her.

HAKIAM: Didn't happen.

MOSHEM: Tomorrow then?

HAKIAM: Never.

MOSHEM: But she was caught in the very act.

HAKIAM: I know.

MOSHEM: And the law . . .

HAKIAM: I know what the law says.

MOSHEM: So I brought all these rocks for nothing?

HAKIAM: We all did.

MOSHEM: Now what am I supposed to do for entertainment?

HAKIAM (*a beat*): You ever hear of a man named Jesus?

MOSHEM: The one they call Christ?

HAKIAM: That's the one.

MOSHEM: What about Him?

HAKIAM: He showed up.

MOSHEM: He was going to stone her too? I didn't think He participated in things like that.

HAKIAM: Sit down. (MOSHEM *sits on the ledge of the well.*) You're right, the woman was caught in the very act. And since the law says she should die, we were prepared to stone her. The whole town. It's not something we look forward to . . . all right (*gives* MOSHEM *a look*), maybe some of us get enjoyment out of that sort of thing, but most of us just do it because the law calls for us to do it. The law is the law.

MOSHEM: Don't misunderstand me. I don't enjoy a stoning either, but I do what I can for the community.

HAKIAM: Of course. We all do. So there we were with our rocks, ready to start hurling them at the woman when along comes this Jesus and says . . .

MOSHEM: Says what?

HAKIAM: He says, "He that is without sin among you, let him first cast a stone at her."

MOSHEM: So did you throw it?

HAKIAM (*gives him another look*): Not me. I'm a long way from perfect.

MOSHEM: Well, did Jesus mean "he that is without sin" or "he that is without *sin*"? There's a difference, you know, between big sins that really bad people do and little ones that everybody does.

HAKIAM: Not to Jesus.

MOSHEM: But murder's not the same as, say, selfishness or pride.

HAKIAM: He doesn't see it that way. To Him, sin is sin.

MOSHEM (*rises*): Then under those rules no one would be able to throw a stone at anybody.

HAKIAM: Exactly. We all stood there and one by one began to walk away.

MOSHEM: Even the Pharisees?

HAKIAM: Even the Pharisees.

MOSHEM: You know, I hear this Jesus can tell you everything about yourself.

HAKIAM: It's His eyes. It's as though He's looking straight into your very soul. He revealed sins that even I didn't know I'd committed. It wasn't a look of condemnation though. I was just overwhelmed with a feeling of unworthiness. Like, who was I to judge another person?

MOSHEM: But the woman had clearly broken the law.

HAKIAM: And Jesus knew that as much as any of us. Don't get me wrong. He didn't condone her sin. He just decided that teaching a lesson in grace and forgiveness was more important than another lesson about the law.

MOSHEM: So now what am I supposed to do with all these rocks?

HAKIAM: Do what some of the rest of us did. We took them down the road a bit and built an altar.

MOSHEM: An altar?

HAKIAM: Yeah, we decided it was better to offer them to God than to throw them at one of His creation.

MOSHEM: Umm . . . Maybe I'll do that. (As he starts to walk offstage, he pauses, takes one of the stones out of his bag, and looks at it.) You know, I sure wouldn't want one of these things hurled at me.

HAKIAM: Yeah, mercy feels a lot better. Guess that's what Jesus was talking about.

MOSHEM: It's a good thing He showed up today after all, huh?

HAKIAM: Not just for that lady's sake. But for all of us.

(They nod and MOSHEM exits.)

Blackout

The Price

Characters:
>MARK
>PHIL
>JOSHUA
>GUARD

Setting:
>There are two settings. SL is a prison interrogation room. SR is a school cafeteria.

Lighting:
>A spotlight is recommended for effect. (If a spotlight is not available, actors on one side of the stage would freeze as the action picks up on the other side of the stage.)

Props:
>Interrogation room scene
>>A chair
>>Loose pages that look like pages of scripture
>>Paper
>>Pen
>
>Cafeteria scene
>>Table and benches or chairs
>>Two trays of food
>>Bible
>>Several other books
>
>Additional props
>>Block of wood, such as was used with a guillotine (should be slightly CS, but blending in with the interrogation room set)

Costumes:
>Jail clothing for JOSHUA
>Guard uniform for GUARD
>Modern-day wear for MARK and PHIL

(Sketch opens with JOSHUA sitting in the chair in the interrogation room. The GUARD is standing over him, holding a pen and paper in his hand. The pages of scripture are in the GUARD's pocket. On the opposite side of the stage PHIL is sitting at a table in the cafeteria. The Bible and his books are next to him. The action begins at SL, the interrogation room.)

GUARD: The choice is simple—sign or we sign for you . . . with your cold dead fingers.

JOSHUA: Do what you have to, but I won't sign.

GUARD: Then you'll die for your God?

JOSHUA: I won't deny Him.

GUARD: Die for someone who doesn't exist?

JOSHUA: He exists whether I live or die.

(JOSHUA *and* GUARD *freeze as action begins SR, cafeteria scene.* PHIL *is at the table eating.* MARK *enters with tray of food in his hand.*)

MARK (*looks around, then to himself*): Oh, great . . . the only available seat is there next to Phil, and all he ever wants to do is talk about God. Boy, you lead a guy to Christ and that's all he can talk about every time he sees you! Why does he think I witnessed to him in private anyway? I don't want the whole school knowing I'm a Christian. I'm not ashamed or anything like that. But if that sort of thing gets out, who knows the persecution I'd have to put up with—laughing behind my back, not telling their off-color jokes around me, not getting invited to certain parties. (*Pause*) I tell you, sometimes this Christian thing is tough.

(*Action freezes SR and resumes SL.*)

GUARD: Deny your God and you'll walk free.

JOSHUA: The only true freedom comes from God.

GUARD (*slaps him across the face*): Don't mock me! Sign!

JOSHUA: Never.

(*Action freezes, then continues SR.*)

MARK (*looks around some more, then frustrated, he approaches* PHIL): Mind if I sit?

PHIL (*obviously pleased to see him*): Hey, Mark! Just the person I wanted to see. You know, I was reading in . . .

MARK: Uh . . . look, Phil, this really isn't the place to be . . .

PHIL: I'll just take a minute. I was reading in . . . (*Takes his Bible from the stack of books next to him and opens it*)

MARK (*quickly and discreetly closing the Bible*): Whoa . . . wait a minute . . . what are you doing, Phil? You can't read that here. Everyone'll see you.

PHIL: So?

MARK: So? (*Thinking quickly*) It could hurt your witness.

PHIL: Reading my Bible will hurt my witness?

MARK: Yeah, it'll scare people, run them off. They'll think you're a fanatic or something. You're a new Christian. You're just gonna have to trust me on this one. Now, come on, put it away. (*He hides the Bible under the table.*)

PHIL: But, Mark, I thought the Bible tells us to hide God's Word in our hearts, not under the table.

MARK: Hearts, under the table . . . who knows which it is with all the different translations floating around. I'll look it up in the original Hebrew. In the meantime, we'll just keep it here. If Mandy Cromwell sees it, she'll never go to the prom with me.

PHIL: I thought you've asked Mandy Cromwell to go out 14 times and she's turned you down 14 times. How's her knowing you're a Christian going to hurt that track record?

MARK: She may have turned me down 14 times, but I think my persistence is paying off. She left off the words "creep," "jerk," and "not on your life" the last time she said no.

PHIL: Have you ever thought she might like the idea that you're a Christian?

MARK: Can't take that chance. The prom's just three weeks away.

(Action freezes and resumes at SL.)

GUARD *(pulls scripture page from his pocket):* We found these in your cell, tucked in a tear in your mattress. Where'd they come from? *(A beat, then)* Where'd they come from?!

JOSHUA: The Bible.

GUARD *(slaps him again):* Don't play me for a fool! I asked you a question! *(Silence, then)* . . . Then they must not be yours. *(Rips them up in pieces and tosses them aside)*

JOSHUA: You may take my life, but you'll never take God's Word from me.

GUARD: I believe I just did.

JOSHUA *(begins quoting scripture to himself, reverently):* "Thy word have I hid in my heart, that I might not sin against thee." "Thy word is a lamp unto my feet, and a light unto my path." "The Lord is my shepherd; I shall not want. He maketh me to lie down in . . ."

GUARD: Enough!

JOSHUA: ". . . to lie down in green pastures: he leadeth me beside the still waters. He restoreth my soul."

(Action freezes and resumes at SR.)

PHIL: I still don't see what's wrong with reading the Bible in public.

MARK: OK, maybe I wouldn't get a date with Mandy Cromwell anyway, but we'd pay for it in some way. Religious persecution. It's rampant.

PHIL: A few snickers behind our back is hardly religious persecution.

MARK: A few snickers? I once had a girl laugh right out loud when I said I went to church on Sundays.

PHIL: Well, that does put you right up there with John the Baptist . . . Stephen . . . Paul . . .

MARK: Exactly. You know what I'm saying then. So, just keep your Bible out of sight and everything'll be fine.

PHIL: Maybe I should just stop reading it altogether.

MARK: No, you should read it. But alone . . . at home . . . in your closet.

PHIL: It's dark in my closet.

MARK: So bring a flashlight. *(Sighs, exasperated)* Baby Christians . . .

(Action stops and resumes SL.)

GUARD: This is your final chance.

JOSHUA: I'm prepared to die for my faith.

GUARD: Then you get your wish. Up! (JOSHUA *rises.* GUARD *shoves him and leads him offstage.)*

(Action resumes on SR.)

PHIL: So, if we don't ever tell anyone that we're Christians, how will they know about God's love for them too?

MARK: We tell them . . . only we do it discreetly, very discreetly, one at a time, every 5 years or so, maybe one every 10 years.

(Action freezes SR. GUARD *leads* JOSHUA *back onstage.* JOSHUA's *hands are now tied behind his back. They stop at the block of wood, which is slightly SC.* JOSHUA *kneels down on his knees and places his head on the block.* GUARD *stands at attention next to him.)*

(Action freezes SL and resumes SR.)

PHIL: So let me see if I've got this right—we shouldn't share our faith because we could get laughed at, people might think we're fanatics, and we might not get a date for the prom?

MARK: Exactly. As Jesus said, "They will . . . persecute you."

PHIL: But if we can't stand up for our faith now . . . here . . . how would we ever be able to do it if we were asked to pay the ultimate price?

MARK: You know, Phil, even for a new Christian, sometimes you just ask too many questions. *(Pause)* You gonna eat that pickle?

Blackout

Mirror, Mirror

Character:
NORMA

Setting:
Bedroom dressing area

Props:
Chair
Dressing table
Mirror
Hair brush
Bible

Costume:
Robe and slippers

(Monologue opens with NORMA *seated in front of the mirror, brushing her hair. She pauses pensively, picks up the Bible, thumbs through it for a few moments, then looks back in the mirror . . .)*

> Mirror, mirror, on the wall
> Who is a Christian, after all?
> On Sunday I am in my pew,
> not sleeping in as others do.

(Her pride slowly gives way to a little self-analysis.)

> But is that works, and do I see
> the faults that lie inside of me?
> If I go on trips to foreign lands,
> if I do my part, if I lend a hand,
> while back at home I show no light
> to those I'm with both day and night?
> Mirror, mirror, on the wall,
> who is a Christian after all?
> If I'm quick to set my neighbor straight,
> yet never tell him of my faith?
> If I pay my tithe, but curse my boss,
> if my heart's grown callous for the lost?
> If discouragement is all I preach
> to those you've given me to reach?
> If I stand too proud, if I feel too sure
> that I need no help, that my heart's so pure?
> If my scripted prayers impress all those
> who hear the words, do you suppose
> that proves that I'm a Christian now?
> Mirror, mirror, tell me how?

If I'm quick to answer when you call,
but judge my brother when he falls?
If I know the rules, but have no heart?
If I promise things I never start?
If I say the words that Christians say,
if I've got it down to the last cliché?
If my love involves no sacrifice?
If I say I'll go, but then think twice?
If I laugh at those who've built on sand,
what part of grace don't I understand?
Mirror, mirror, on the wall,
God sees the real me after all.

Blackout